Realtor for GOD

Realtor for GOD

It's about the mission not the commission

By Rene Compton

Xulon Press

Xulon Press
2301 Lucien Way #415
Maitland, FL 32751
407.339.4217
www.xulonpress.com

© 2017 by Rene Compton

All rights reserved solely by the author. The author guarantees all contents are original and do not infringe upon the legal rights of any other person or work. No part of this book may be reproduced in any form without the permission of the author. The views expressed in this book are not necessarily those of the publisher.

This nonfiction book is based on my memory of actual events. Some of the names, places, and identifying characteristics have been changed to maintain the anonymity of those involved.

Scripture quotations taken from the King James Version (KJV)–*public domain.*

Printed in the United States of America.

ISBN-13: 9781545614266

Acknowledgments

I have been inspired by so many and blessed by the one and only God in heaven with an amazing husband and two of the most precious sons that any mother could ever have. I would like to thank my late grandmother, Ethel Priest, for being such a wonderful prayer warrior for our family. She set an example of how to love people and how to love our Father in heaven. My dad was a wonderful man with a heart of kindness, and everyone loved him. He struggled for years as God tugged on his heart, but God never gave up on him, and neither did my grandmother. She kept him covered in prayer daily. I have followed in my grandmother's footsteps and kept my sons covered in prayer as well.

I would like to thank my dear sister for her continuous help and support in my life. She is never too busy to help me, and I know she is always there for me. What a precious sister—and the best realtor I know. I would also like to thank Don Newman, the Director of Acquisitions for Xulon Press, where I was blessed to work for the past ten years. It was hard to give up this environment when God reassigned me on a new journey. Don kept us all covered with prayer and would often request prayer for our children and other family members. It was such a protected environment, and it was all because of his love for God and others. His example has prepared me for my new assignment as a realtor for God.

I would also like to thank my precious authors for sharing their publishing journeys with me over the past ten years. I was inspired daily by those God sent to me. I realize the impact a book can have on lives, and that is why I have written this book. I hope it might be your inspiration to write your journey or sing your song. Don't hide your light to the world under a bush. Shine it bright on the darkness in the world!

Photo taken by Rene Compton of the Ponce Inlet Lighthouse.

Table of Contents

Introduction xiii
Chapter 1 – One Day by the Sea 1
Chapter 2 – The Call 5
Chapter 3 – Deborah and Me 9
Chapter 4 – Juggling Act 19
Chapter 5 – Handshake of Encouragement 25
Chapter 6 – The Mouse Key 29
Chapter 7 – The Birdhouse 35
Chapter 8 – Time to Go 41
Chapter 9 – Peace in the Valley 55
Chapter 10 – Focused on the Mission 63
Chapter 11 - Don't Ask Why; Just Go! 71
Chapter 12 – Rescue 410 .77
Conclusion 83

Introduction

I want you to use this book as inspiration and motivation to help you get out of your bed and do what God is calling you to do. I am beginning this book at 3 a.m., and yes, I got out of bed to write it. It is very easy in life to get too comfortable and procrastinate in what God is calling you to do. The joy comes when you obey the calling. Your journey is waiting, so don't delay and miss the life that God has waiting for you. My prayer is that this book and its stories will give insight of just how important it is for you to trust God with your life.

Life is a gift from God, and gifts are intended to bring joy and happiness. I hope we're in agreement with this statement. If you don't agree with this statement, you probably won't enjoy this book. If you do agree, this book will have an amazing impact on your life because I believe God provided the resources and inspiration for every chapter.

Photograph taken by Rene Compton
of the New Smyrna Beach sunrise on August 19, 2016

Chapter 1

One Day by the Sea

I arrived early to pray that morning by the sea and started to write a message to God in the sand. I love the ocean, and it has always been my dream to live by the sea. Peace floods my spirit whenever I hear the ocean and see the waves. As I sit by the shore, I always write messages in the sand to God—and this is how my journey in real estate began.

It is very important to me that this book make a difference in your life and the lives of others by helping to answer a very important question: Why is there life? Tuck that thought away for now; we will revisit it soon.

On this particular day, I felt inspired to write a message to the people in the large condo behind me. Most of the time I would write "Jesus loves you!" I continued to visit this place at the beach and pray, and I continually saw answered prayers in my life and in the lives of others. God had given me an amazing job with a Christian publisher, and I daily thanked Him for His blessings and provision. So you can imagine what I felt and the questions I asked on the day He told me He wanted me to sell real estate. *Why, God, would You want me to give up what I am currently doing? Am I not doing a good job helping those Christian writers tell their stories?*

It still brings tears to my eyes when I remember how I felt that day He was redirecting my path. I thought I had let the Lord down. I even explained to God that real estate seemed so worldly, and I just didn't understand why He was asking me to leave this wonderful, safe place with all my friends to go after a worldly job. I know that God knows best, so that meant I had to leave my beloved job. Maybe I could do both, I reasoned. You know, hang on to the security of my current job and see if I could get my real estate license. My head was spinning with questions like *How am I going to do this?* and *What if I'm not good at real estate?* What if? Lots of what ifs—along with stress and more work to do now to get my license. Okay, Lord, I trust You! Show me how to begin.

I returned home and reached out to my sister because she is a real estate broker in Georgia. She gave me information on how to get my license. She also told me that real estate is not an easy job and has some bad hours with lot of risks. Dear me, instead of feeling better about my new assignment, I was feeling very nervous. I kept reminding myself of what God had placed on my heart that day at the beach. I did not have the time availability to go to a school, so I chose to do an online course to prepare for the state exam. I worked hard, listening to tapes, watching online videos, and learning everything I could possibly learn about real estate. I finished the online course and took the online exam—and failed. I then had to wait a designated period of time before I could retake the test online. I studied more and took the test again—and yes, I failed it again!

At this point I was really discouraged, but I was not going to give up because I had invested a lot of time and money with the materials and testing. So I signed up for another online course, and this time I passed. I now had my course exam certificate, and I could take the state exam. *Oh my goodness!* I thought. *If I had a difficult time with the online course exam, how in the world will I pass the state exam?*

I went ahead and scheduled my state exam as soon as possible because I did not want to forget what I had already worked so hard to learn. Working to attain my real estate license while working my current job was a challenging endeavor. I kept reminding myself that God wanted me to do this. Didn't He? I questioned myself time and time again—thinking maybe I just *thought* He wanted me to do this. Maybe I had felt that way because I love to look at houses.

Despite the doubt that kept returning, God encouraged me to stay on the path because of my deep longing to do His will. I realized it was His plan and not mine; I'd had plenty of confirmations on the journey. Confirmations will keep you focused on the path and the journey. Just like road signs that tell you that you only have so many miles to your destination, these confirmations from God really help you not to pull off the road of life but to stay steady on the journey. Watch for the confirmations from God in your life that will help to direct your path. They will be there if you just take the time and open your mind to see them. You must discern His will.

Chapter 2

The Call

Little did I realize I was about to answer a telephone call that would positively impact my life in more ways than one. My work phone rang, and when I picked it up the woman on the line said she had written a children's book she would like to get published. She went on to say that she had written the book years ago but just did not know what to do to fulfill her dream of becoming a published author. She found out about me through a mutual contact who gave her my name and number. The Orlando-based publishing company that employed me allowed me to work from home two days a week because I live at the coast, more than fifty miles away from Orlando. So the author, who also lived near me, asked if she could meet me at my home instead of driving to Orlando.

For obvious reasons, I had never agreed to meet a

writer at my home but would typically meet at a local restaurant or coffee shop. This time, however, I made an exception, and we agreed upon a time to meet. The following week when we met, I found out that she lived just a few streets over from me and was living with her daughter temporarily until she could find a house to purchase. Although she was working with a realtor, she had been unable to find anything in her budget and was getting frustrated. I thought to myself, *It would be nice if I had my license because I could perhaps help her find a house.* I also shared with her some of my personal journey about how God had helped my husband and me to find our home.

The following week—which happened to be the very week my state exam was scheduled—she returned to make her final decision about publishing her book. She told me again that she really needed to find another realtor, and I gave her the information for the realtor who had helped us with our house. My sister (the realtor) encouraged me to tell her that I was getting my license. But I felt too much stress to even share with her that I was currently trying to get my real estate license. The memory of my struggles with the online course exam prevented me from pursuing this real estate opportunity that literally knocked at my door.

After she signed up with me to publish her book, we discussed guidelines for submitting her finished manuscript as soon as possible. Ironically, her book was titled *Why Do Birds Fly South for the Winter?* I would be working with snowbirds soon if I passed my state exam. This wonderful book about birds had a comedic twist including snowbirds' adventures moving south to escape the cold weather. I could see that God was giving me insider knowledge for my new adventure too. Later I will also share how God connected me with this woman named Deborah for reasons that extend beyond helping her to publish a book.

I studied for the rest of that week, and then the day of the state exam arrived. I was so nervous, and I was making my last review of the math portion with the online videos early that morning. Initially I had decided not to go to the beach to pray that morning, but I knew I had to talk to God because more than ever before I needed the peace that came from time spent with Him by the sea. So I decided to go and pray.

I arrived at the exam office just minutes before my scheduled testing time. I was all the more nervous due to the fact that I had difficulty finding the exact location of the place with only minutes to spare. After locking my personal items away, I made my way to the exam room—walking alone but knowing I was not alone. God was with me. The test came up on the screen, and I felt good about the first few questions. When I came to questions I did not feel confident about, I was able to recognize clues that helped determine the correct answers. I knew God was helping me with the test. Surprisingly, it was the easiest test I have ever taken. I always struggled with tests in high school and college, so it was amazing that I knew the answers and felt so confident. I finished my test and knew I had passed before they graded it. When they officially announced that I had passed, it was an amazing confirmation! By the grace of God, I was now ready to embark upon an exciting new career with new learning experiences. I was reminded once again that I can always hold onto His words.

Philippians 4:13
I can do all things through Christ which strengtheneth me.

Chapter 3

Deborah and Me

I needed to follow up with Deborah about getting her book published. Before calling her, however, I wanted to touch base with the realtor I had previously referred her to. To my surprise, the realtor thought I was helping Deborah because I had gotten my license and we both worked for the same real estate company. I did not want to take business away from my coworker, but she insisted that I help find Deborah a home since I was the one who referred Deborah to her in the first place. I graciously accepted the opportunity and was now on the first mission of my new assignment from God.

Excited, I picked up the phone and told Deborah that I could assist her with publishing, but I also could help her find a new home.

I could see how God had directed both our paths. We both felt His peace as we searched and prayed for the home that God had waiting. I was amazed at how God had brought the two assignments together: publishing and real estate. Others were also amazed at how God had arranged it all. I was so encouraged by the possibilities. Yes, I could serve Him in this new assignment. I never saw it coming. I juggled both responsibilities gladly and enjoyed every long night I spent finding Deborah's new home while helping her to become a published author.

God answered quickly, and we found the perfect house. I will never forget that day. It still brings tears to my eyes as I recall the look on her face when she saw the home. I arrived before she did, and when I unlocked the door I knew it was the house we had been looking for. I could not wait for Deborah to see it. Upon her arrival, I ran outside to prepare her for what she was about to see. When I opened the front door, she stood in the doorway and was very quiet. I asked her what she thought, and she appeared overwhelmed for a moment. She responded, "I cannot believe that God would give me such a beautiful home." I told her it was hers and that I would do whatever I could to get the house and the furniture. We ran through it like little girls in a playhouse, so excited with what our Father in heaven had shown us this day.

The house was over budget, but I knew God would make a way. Keep in mind, I was a new realtor and not feeling very confident in my new role, but I was confident in what God could do. I kept her encouraged that God was going to help us and reminded her that the house was hers. I stepped out on a limb, but I knew that God was holding my hand. I couldn't do this, but God could.

This was the beginning. I had no idea what was next, but I knew I had to get the contract written up and signed before this house was gone. God always sends you the help you need, and, wow, He sent me my sister Rhoda—the best helper ever! She owns her own real estate company in my hometown in Georgia, and she is the best realtor I know. She patiently answered all my questions and concerns. What a wonderful blessing to have her available to guide me with her expertise and years of experience. God worked out every detail to help me excel in my new career.

I went from being a knowledgeable publishing consultant and author coach to someone who struggled to attain knowledge in an unfamiliar field that requires so much legal expertise. The company I chose to work for offered a very extensive training program, and I was thankful for this opportunity. So I chose to focus on the positives and kept reminding myself of that day of the final test and how God revealed the answers to me! He is all-knowing, so why did I need to worry? My first day on the job as a realtor, God sent my dear friend Lily. She took me under her wing and showed me the ropes of having a successful open house. We enjoyed our long talks and shared many special times together. Lily moved away just a few months later, and I still miss her smiling face.

In spite of my challenges, I decided to focus on what I did know instead of what I didn't know. This gave me a better perspective on my new challenge. Soon I realized that God had totally prepared me for this new assignment, and that He would always send me the help I needed.

The fear quickly vanished after I came to the full realization that God had been preparing me for this adventure for years.

- I had already sold five of our own personal homes over the years with flyers and newspaper ads. Only one was sold with the use of technology.
- I had worked for one of the largest title companies in Florida as a helpdesk representative for three years and was trained in mortgage closing software.
- My background was in computer science, and I had published a book called *Unlock Technology with the Computer Puppets*.

- I had worked as a publishing sales consultant for the past ten years, and this position helped me to develop my ability to close sales and make dreams come true for writers who wanted to get their books published.

I am now making dreams come true for people who want to purchase their dream homes, and I count it a privilege to have had the opportunity over the years to hear what God has done in the lives of the authors I served. Some of these authors were missionaries who encountered dangers I could only read about. Others had compelling stories to tell, but were challenged in writing their testimonies. So I would provide practical coaching tips to get them motivated enough to complete their manuscripts. Sometimes I would pray for them over the phone, and sometimes they would pray for my own family and me. I tried to always keep them encouraged so they could write their book or fulfill God's purpose in general. All they needed to do was pray and stay dedicated to completing the work. God is the creator of all things. He can and will help you fulfill what He is calling you to do.

I knew that it was important to share my journey as a realtor for God in a book. I hope it is an encouragement to all to do what God has called you to do. I hope you can see from my experience how God guided and directed my footsteps. I also hope you will see that although it might be a long journey that will not be easy, you should search for your purpose and avoid getting detoured from your path.

Galatians 6:9
And let us not be weary in well doing: for in
due season we shall reap, if we faint not.

My author and very first client in real estate was about to have a signed bilateral contract on her first home. The listing realtor and I worked together to get all parties in agreement, and late on a Friday night we received the good news. The sellers had accepted Deborah's offer, and we had a signed bilateral contract. Deborah and I were ecstatic but also nervous; yet God's hand was upon it all. Then the day came for my very first closing and the beginning of my new career. I was a realtor for God, and this was my assigned mission. I also quickly realized that it is about the mission, not the commission. I never saw this coming, and I could not see how I might serve Him even more in my new assignment—but it was now becoming crystal clear as Deborah moved into her new home.

Since I was a little girl I had dreamed of being an artist. Could I possibly now get to combine my lifelong desire to be an artist with this new assignment from God? I began painting a very special gift for Deborah's new home, one that I felt reflected how God had answered our prayers. I had previously told her about my experience of writing in the sand at the beach and how God had given me my new assignment. How I questioned it at first but now understood how I could be used by God in my new assignment for His glory. The painting depicted the words "Welcome Home" written in the sand, with the ocean rushing in upon the shore. I was so excited to let her see the painting. I quickly called her to see when I might visit her.

Deborah was still moving in when I delivered her housewarming gift. She loved the painting. We both rejoiced about how God had taken care of everything. Her son would soon be moving in with her when he finished school up north, and they had this beautiful home to share.

Again, God confirmed that I was indeed a realtor for Him. I cried and cried with joy and thankfulness. Let this be a reminder that if He lays it upon your heart to do something, don't question it. Be obedient and trusting because there is a purpose far beyond what we can see with our own eyes. His plan is always better than ours!

Psalm 16:11
Thou wilt shew me the path of life: in thy presence is fulness of joy; at thy right hand there are pleasures for evermore.

Acrylic Painting - Welcome Home by Rene Compton

Chapter 4

Juggling Act

As the months went by, I was still driving to Orlando and trying to juggle both real estate and publishing, but it was becoming more difficult to keep up with both responsibilities. I had held an open house on the weekend at one of the larger condo complexes in New Smyrna Beach, where I met a nice couple from Orlando who were looking for a condo directly on the beach. I scheduled a day off from work and met up with them at the real estate office to start our tour of several condos I believed might interest them.

One of the condos we viewed was located on the beach where I always went to pray. This special spot was where God had answered a lot of prayers and given me directions. It was where He placed it on my heart to write the messages so the people in this condo could see them. Later, after previewing the condos, I was talking with Deborah about her book publishing, and she asked me how the real estate was going. I told her that I got to show the condo where I went to pray. I mentioned the name of the condominium in our conversation, and she said that the lady she was taking care of lived there and that she herself was there on a weekly basis. I stood amazed once more at how God was directing my path. Just like a puzzle, He continued to give me pieces of this amazing journey. I anticipate the completed picture puzzle as a successful realtor for God. I will continue to work with one piece at a time until it makes a beautiful picture of my life doing God's work.

August was a very intense month in my publishing job, and I put forth great effort to sign as many authors as possible to meet our annual goal. I also wanted to earn enough money to purchase a cruise for my family. We had not been on a vacation together in four years. God knows the desires of our hearts, and I trusted that He would provide a way for me to do this for the family. Every day my husband would ask me if I was in the top three on the sales team contest, because only the top three bonuses would provide enough money to pay for the cruise. If I didn't win, it was going to be unrealistic to purchase this vacation. I believed in my heart that God was going to provide, so I purchased a seven-day cruise for all six family members a couple of weeks after the contest started. I felt peace about my decision, but my husband was a little bit concerned. Make that a lot concerned.

Almost every day after work he would ask me where I was in the contest, and almost every time he asked I had slipped lower on the board. I told him I had peace about purchasing the cruise and that God was going to provide. It was more than just a cruise; it was a chance for our family to be together away from work and the struggles of everyday life. I wasn't sure, but I held onto the promise that God would provide.

On the final day of the contest I was not in the top three, but I still had peace that it would be okay. One week after the contest ended, we received our commission statements, and it brought me to tears. Even though I didn't win the contest, I had collected enough that month to pay for the cruise in full! It wasn't the way I thought God would provide, but He provided and answered my prayer. My family and I would be going on a cruise in January together. My husband and family were so excited about the cruise.

Meanwhile I continued to thank God for His provision, even as I struggled to keep both responsibilities covered. Praying at the beach one day, I asked God what He wanted me to do while I was writing in the sand. Should I leave publishing: yes or no? I opened my Bible to read, and God revealed the answer—it was *yes*. The Lord wanted me to leave this wonderful job of almost ten years and start a new career with an unknown salary. Leave my safe environment with my praying coworkers and boss and fly solo! So far, I had only made one sale in real estate.

Then I asked God when He wanted me to leave. Don't ever ask if you don't want to know, because if He tells you, you better be prepared to go! While reading my Bible, I was a bit overwhelmed when I felt the Lord directing me to leave *the first month and fifteenth day.* I asked, *Oh, dear Lord, are You sure?* All the way home I wrestled with how bad it would look for me to give my notice the day after I returned from the cruise. What in the world would I do? Would I need to give notice before I left?

As I sat at my desk at home, it came to me that this was probably a Jewish calendar, so I reached out to one of my coworkers through instant messaging and asked him when the first month and fifteenth day was. He, of course, had no idea why I was asking at the time. He asked me, "What year?" I responded with 2017. He is a messianic Jew, so I knew he would be able to give me the correct date. He announced that it was April 10. What a relief and peace of mind! Hopefully I could juggle it all until April, and with the family cruise in January it was a wonderful plan that God had provided.

God was about to open a new door of opportunity at my next open house. This would provide needed encouragement for the journey I was about to embark on April 10, 2017.

Numbers 33:1-3 KJV

1 These *are* the journeys of the children of Israel, which went forth out of the land of Egypt with their armies under the hand of Moses and Aaron.

2 And Moses wrote their goings out according to their journeys by the commandment of the LORD: and these *are* their journeys according to their goings out.

3 And they departed from Rameses in the first month, on the fifteenth day of the first month; on the morrow after the passover the children of Israel went out with an high hand in the sight of all the Egyptians.

SUNRISE WALKER

REALTOR FOR GOD

Chapter 5

Handshake of Encouragement

As I hosted my next open house, I opened the door and welcomed the two women standing in the doorway. One of the ladies, named Rebecca, reached out and shook my hand and instantly asked me to help her find her vacation home. I was so excited and began my search right away. We worked together over the next two weeks. She found a house that she was very interested in and was ready to place a bid, but the house already had a bid on it. Her husband, Jack, was not as excited about the home as she was, so they decided not to place a backup bid on the property, but continued to look at other options.

Within weeks another house came on the market, and Jack thought it was a great house, but Rebecca still was undecided. Every time she visited down at the dock, the dolphins and manatees would be swimming in the water. Once they even saw an alligator. They both felt good about the area, and God already had a vacation home picked out for them. They soon signed a contract, which was accepted. We were trying to close by Christmas, and it looked like it was going to happen.

This home was going to be a getaway from work and stress for the two of them and their daughter. At the closing, I found out that Jack and Rebecca had been through a very difficult time recently. Jack had lost his daughter from a previous marriage. She was in her early twenties when she died. He was currently in counseling trying to deal with his grief. I knew God had brought this couple to me and that I was to bring God's message to this grief-stricken man. I wanted to let him know that God loved him and that it was going to be okay. On the day of the closing, as we were parting ways in the parking lot, God gave me the opportunity to pray with him. As I hugged them both while saying goodbye, I said a special prayer of hope for Jack.

This vacation home offered a new opportunity for them to enjoy life again. I know that God arranged for this woman to walk through the door of my open house that day because it was ultimately His purpose for me to encourage this precious husband and wife. God arranged a friendship that I will always treasure. I continue to pray for them and for the peace that only

God can bring to this family. I created a special painting of the river depicting a manatee swimming near the dock—just a small reminder of how much I appreciate our new friendship.

Matthew 5:4
Blessed are they that mourn: for they shall be comforted.

Acrylic Painting - Manatee by Rene Compton

Chapter 6

The Mouse Key

This chapter holds a special place in my heart because my youngest son, Spencer, referred this family to me—a family whose baby had her first birthday the week before they closed on their new home. I can't wait to tell you how God found the perfect house for them.

We met on a Saturday and viewed a lot of homes. It was a real marathon of house hunting. We thought we had found the perfect one and rushed back to the office to put together a contract. The couple, Dave and Mary, loved the home, and it had the most unique door key—shaped like a guitar. I had never seen a key like this. We prayed about it at the office, and they left with high hopes. Before I could submit the offer, I found out the property was pending with another offer. The realtor said we could submit a backup offer. I called to give them what we perceived to be bad news at the time. They were both very disappointed, especially Dave. He wanted the house with the guitar key, and it was going to be hard for him to move on from this one. They decided not to make a backup offer.

The following Monday they sent me several texts with different houses they had found in a nearby community. Still heartbroken over the guitar house, they were trying to find a replacement. I knew this replacement was not going to be difficult for God because He is all-knowing. It was about to turn into an amazing journey that we would all be talking about for a very long time.

I was still working in Orlando and attempted to schedule all the home viewings on my lunch hour that day. There were several on the list of text messages from Dave and Mary.

When I arrived to meet them that evening, I was delighted to see their sweet baby in the car. Instead of switching out the car seat, we went in their car. We made our first stop on the list; it was not definitely not the guitar house. Not even close. We visited two more, and then we arrived at our final house, one that was not on their list and one that would be the answer to my prayers.

On their list was a house that was no longer available on this street, but I found another one that would serve as a replacement. Let me reword that: I felt that God found this house on that same street. We had run from house to house, and by the time we arrived at this one it was getting dark. That sweet baby was with us the entire time as we visited one home after another, held in her mother's arms. At the front door, I leaned forward to send the signal from my cell phone to open the door. The lock box fell open in my hand, and then I saw the Mouse Key. I lifted it up so the little girl could see it, and she responded with the most beautiful smile. I didn't even have to open the door to know that this was the house for them.

As I opened the door, it was like God shined a light on this home. Walking from room to room, we all knew that this was indeed the home for them. I locked the door with the Mouse Key and walked out into the driveway with them, praying that God would provide a way to get this home if this was the house He had for them. God will always keep the light shining upon your path when you pray for direction. I wanted them to know that I only wanted what God wanted them to have.

I have learned that God leaves you a well-lit path to follow on your journey with Him, but you have to open your eyes as you walk on it. There are directional signs everywhere if you will stay focused on Him. It is important that you discern and not get detoured down a dark and lonely road. The enemy tries to detour us from God's goodness and the path He has planned for us. Sometimes we feel that God has redirected our path, and we want what we want, when we want it. But this can be a very dangerous place to be on your life's journey. If you don't feel the peace of the Holy Spirit on your journey, you could be on a detoured path by the enemy and be all by your lonesome. Just like a sheep—if a wolf can get that little sheep away from its shepherd, he can attack and devour it. Stay close to the Father as you navigate through life's journey so that you don't get detoured and devoured.

Oh, how sweet to be on the path that God has planned. I believe these new homeowners would tell you the same, that it was a very easy process. What a joy it was to meet Dave and Mary at the home during the inspection and final walkthrough before closing. When the closing came, God continued to bless with additional money that was unexpectedly received at the closing table. Finally, the listing realtor arrived with the key. Yes, the Mouse Key!

What a wonderful feeling it was to know that this family now had such a beautiful home to live in, but even better was that they knew who had provided it for them. I rushed home to finish the painting I had started. I had decided to paint a picture of two mice holding the special key for the little girl's room. When I thought I was finished, the painting still did not feel complete. I decided to write the word "BLESSED!" on the painting—hoping it would be a reminder of just how blessed they are to have God in their lives.

Chapter 7

The Birdhouse

While helping a young married couple find a home, I was reminded that sometimes God brings reinforcement for the journey. This young couple was going to be my strength for this closing, and their faith would shine all the way across the finish line. It was a blessing to help them find their first home. The wife, Emily, was one of our prayer group warriors at the Christian publishing company where I still worked. She had asked me to help them find their first home.

We met up one Saturday to begin our long day of looking at the Orlando market. We had several areas of Orlando to view, and we began our journey in Winter Springs. I got to our first house early and looked over the amazing patio and pool area. The ledge that extended out from the kitchen window reminded me of our family home with a pool and how my two sons would come up to the window and order food and drinks while they were playing in the pool. They would run around to the kitchen and pay me with kisses that felt like a butterfly had lit upon my face. It was like an old movie playing in my mind, and I longed to see them standing by that window again with nothing to do but play in the pool. What a wonderful home this would be for a young family, I thought to myself.

I came back in the house to wait on the couple to arrive. As I glanced over at the counter I saw the home flyers spread out on the counter. I thought it was strange that the flyers were spread out over the counter, so I put on my glasses and then realized that the flyers were of different houses. The homeowner was a house flipper, and he had other properties that would soon be on the market. What I was not expecting to see on one of the flyers was our previous family home—the same home I was just daydreaming about with the pool and the window ledge server.

My heart was overwhelmed, and I could not hold back the tears. I was texting my two sons a photo of the flyer of our previous home when Emily and her husband arrived to view the house. I was so thankful that it was my precious coworker because I knew she would understand how God had touched my heart that morning. When she walked through the door, I explained to her why I was crying. She hugged me, and that was the beginning of our house hunting journey for their first home.

We found a home that Emily and Mike loved that first day, but there were already several offers on the house, and even though they did not get this house their faith did not waver. They continued to search, and soon we narrowed down the search to an area closer to his job. After seeing how fast everything was selling, these two knew that once they found the house they would need to move quickly. But they would not be moving without prayer or direction. Then we found the house, and I asked Mike to pray as we stood in the home. It was not long before we were writing a contract and beginning negotiations.

Late that night after submitting the offer, Emily sent me a text message about her concerns over the house and how her mom felt that they might be able to find a better house for a better price. I prayed about it, and before the sun came up the next morning, Emily was at peace with their decision. Emily and Mike already knew the current market and its limitations. Most of the homes were sold or pending before we viewed them, but most of all they had prayed in that home, and they had to trust the peace God had given them that day.

I guess you are wondering why I titled this chapter "The Birdhouse." It is an amazing story how God used their soon-to-be neighbor's birdhouse to bring such joy to me, but also peace to one of my coworkers. We returned to look at the house one more time, and then Emily and I saw the birdhouse standing in her backyard. It was a "See Rock City" birdhouse! How did we not see this the week before? Emily and I stared at it over the fence. My cell phone battery was dead, so I asked Emily to take a picture for our friend at work who in the coming weeks would be moving to Chattanooga, Tennessee—which is very close to Rock City.

Although I had lived in Florida for over twenty years, I had never seen one of these types of birdhouses. You see them all the time in Georgia and Tennessee. I had already shared with our friend at work who was moving to Chattanooga that my sister was a realtor in Dalton, Georgia, and that if she ever needed someone, she could reach out to her for help on a personal level. My sister would be happy to help her until her mom could get there from Florida. Her mom was so thankful that she had a connection to someone closer to her new job location.

The following Monday my manager was standing at my desk when my coworker who was moving to Chattanooga came looking for him, not me. When I saw her, I instantly thought of the birdhouse photo. I quickly called Emily to remind her to send the picture to her and to send me a copy too. When I got the photo, I just had to have a See Rock City birdhouse. I Googled it and soon found it online. I ordered it that very day. A couple of days later I received the tracking information, which confirmed that the order was being shipped from my hometown of Dalton, Georgia. What are the chances? I now look out my back window at my birdhouse, and it always reminds me of Emily and her husband and our journey with God finding their first home.

Every step of the way we were challenged: during the inspection, then with the appraisal; and just days before the closing the numbers didn't match. It was like running an obstacle course and a long marathon to the finish line. I am just thankful that I was running this marathon with such an amazing young Christian couple, because we could pray all the way across the finish line. I learned a lot during this experience, and the birdhouse in my backyard is a beautiful reminder.

Photo taken by Rene Compton – My birdhouse

Chapter 8

Time to Go

*R*emember that amazing job I really did not want to give up. It was time to give notice after ten wonderful years. Giving up a job is easy if you don't like it, or if it doesn't pay well, but I was very satisfied with this job. God always knows best, so I figured He must have something even better for me. Yes, I looked forward to not having to drive all the way to Orlando from New Smyrna Beach on the most dangerous highway in the US. Three days a week, I made a three-hour commute with all the construction and traffic delays on I-4. Almost every day that I traveled on this highway I would see a broken-down vehicle or an accident. My husband was extremely concerned and prayed for my safety on this road where daily crashes seemed inevitable. I had been making the commute for almost four years since we moved, and it gave me a lot of time to talk to God. When I was trying to get my real estate license, I would listen to my MP3 player on my way there and back home again. God uses all things for the good, so even when I was on the road I saw His hand upon my life, directing me and keeping me safe.

My first such encounter after the move to the beach happened early one morning. Initially, it appeared to be an ordinary day, but it was not going to be. Later that morning I would find myself praising God again and again for His protection.

On Monday morning when I got to my car, the gas gauge was on empty. My husband normally filled up the car after driving it on Sunday, but for some reason he didn't get around to it. That proved to be a blessing this particular morning because the delay was going to work in my favor. That is how I have come to understand and not get frustrated when I am late going somewhere. I don't ever like to be late, so I will show up early just to avoid the stress. But when I have made all reasonable efforts to get somewhere on time and am delayed, I trust that God is perhaps protecting me from something or someone.

This morning confirmed to me that the empty tank was no accident, but His divine plan. When I reached I-4, things were moving along, but they quickly came to an abrupt halt. Highway warning signs read "Crash I-4 westbound all lanes closed." I was almost to the river bridge but was too far to exit and go another route. All I could do was wait. It was a bad accident from what I was hearing on the radio. I sat on I-4 for over two hours that morning with helicopters flying overhead. I was so close to the accident that they redirected the traffic over to Highway 17-92. The news channels were there waiting when the first cars directly behind the fatal accident came off the ramp. The person in the car in front of me was being interviewed on camera. I was pretty shaken up and relieved they did not interview me but let me pass by off the ramp.

The traffic was still bumper-to-bumper on this road. I let a truck out of a side road and was sitting in traffic behind it. I'm not sure what happened, but I bumped the back of this truck, and unfortunately it had a big trailer hitch on the back. My car was just a few months old so this was sickening. The guy got out of his truck and said his truck was fine, but my car did not look good. I could not sit in traffic any longer, and I concluded that I was not supposed to drive to work that day. I called my manager and told him if I made it up to the next road, I was turning around and going back home. He agreed and I went back home with my front bumper messed up. I don't think I even looked at it before I got home.

Thankfully I arrived home and rushed to get busy on my work phone. I was still not fully functioning after my long morning ride and bumper ordeal. Suddenly it occurred to me that I had a tag cover that I had never put on my car. I rushed outside to get it from my trunk, and to my amazement it covered the hole in my bumper. I was so thankful for the Band-Aid that God had already provided for the car. If you look at my car you will not see the hole, but I know it is there and it's okay—because it will always serve as a reminder of how God protected me that day. I was blessed to get to return home to my family, but I learned later that morning that a young woman did not survive the accident on that highway and would not be returning home from work that day. A baby would be without its mother. My heart was saddened.

As I continued to drive this dangerous road each day, I always thought of the young woman who lost her life that morning. She was a nurse at a local hospital and had a small child. Someone else was closer to the accident than I was, and it would change his career choice in life. I always had lunch with my best friend Sarah at work, and her daughter worked there at the publishing company as our receptionist. Her fiancé was the first person to reach the young woman who was killed in the accident that dreadful morning. Her fiancé had been training to be a firefighter and EMT. This accident would change all that for him!

The young mother was on the westbound lane several cars in front of me, but the dump truck that hit her was on the eastbound lane right in front of this young man when the dump truck tire experienced a blowout and the truck went across the median and directly into the westbound lane of traffic, where the truck hit this young mother's car. The young man who was training to be a firefighter and EMT jumped into action and ran to her assistance, but it was too late. His fears were compounded when he saw the baby seat in the backseat, and he quickly searched to see if the baby was with her. Later it was found out that she had dropped the baby off before she got on I-4. This was the last time she would see her baby here on earth, and it still weighs on my heart; it also weighed on the heart of this young man. He spoke about it often with our receptionist and decided that he could not deal with these kinds of experiences every day. He knew he could not continue working as a firefighter and EMT. Everyone who knew him felt it was best because it had affected him so much emotionally. It had also affected me emotionally, and I did not even see the young woman and certainly did not check her pulse that day.

Realtor for God

On I-4 you just never know what will happen. I continued to see accident after accident, and I always prayed that the people were safe as I passed by them on the highway. On another day, I came close to being involved in one of those accidents, and it started with a blown-out tire on a lawncare trailer. I was in the fast lane, and so was this lawncare company pulling a trailer packed full of large riding mowers and equipment. I was talking with my son Ryan on my cell and had just told him goodbye and that I loved him. All I remember is the trailer turning sideways in front of my car and the parts of the tire hitting my car and skidding off the roof of my car. The driver was trying to get it under control, and I prayed that he would be able to stop. He had no choice but to move over to the slow lane and off the side of the road. Thankfully there were no cars in those lanes. Praise God, the truck finally came to a stop beside the road, and I was shaking at the wheel.

My phone rang and it was my youngest son, Spencer. He could tell that something was wrong; I just started to cry and told him what had just happened. He told me in a very reassuring voice that everything was going to be okay and that God was with me. He was exactly right; God had never left my side. Even though it was a scary day, it was a blessing to hear my precious son put his trust in God. What a wise young man. I am so proud of him. I soon began to focus on all that had gone right instead of all that had gone wrong. Today, I will go out of my way not to be behind any trailers!

Proverbs 22:6
> Train up a child in the way he should go: and when he is old, he will not depart from it.

Finally, I was down to two days left at work, and the team had arranged a farewell lunch together. I arrived early because traffic was good that Thursday. I decided that I would make a new prayer board that morning. This was my responsibility each month, and my manager had asked me to take care of it one more time before I left. This was nothing more than a big white board, but it held some precious names and prayers on it. I have one at home now too! This board would fill up in one month, so I always took a picture before I erased it, and then we would begin a new month.

I had erased the board and was adding something special for my final month as the caretaker of the board—a photo of the picnic table behind our offices before we moved to our new office building. This was a special place to several of us because a lot of answered prayer had happened at this picnic table. Several of us would meet for prayer time and ask God for direction along with many other requests. We had returned a few times and again experienced that peace from this place of prayer. I printed out a new photo of the picnic table. Meanwhile, one of my coworkers and precious friends came by, and she appeared to be in a rush when I was taping the picnic table on the board. I wondered why she had acted so strangely about this being on the board. I even thought maybe she did not want me to put tape on the white board. Within the hour I knew why she had acted so strangely about the board, and it had nothing to do with tape on the board.

That very morning as I was finishing the board, one of my other dear friends (also a coworker) came up and told me that God had a word for me that she wanted to share. She told me that all the extra care and kindness I had given the authors over the years would be returned to me in real estate. I was known for even using my personal time to go the extra mile to help authors who lacked the technical computer skills or other resources to complete their projects. What these authors did have, however, was an amazing passion to write about what God had done in their lives in order to share their stories with others. How was I to say no or refuse to help them when their messages could potentially reach the heart of lost souls? I felt so blessed that God placed this word on my friend's heart for me—letting me know that

I would reap great blessings in real estate partly due to my caring nature in my publishing job.

On a different occasion, another friend (also a former coworker at the publishing company) encouraged me by stating that he felt the simple secret to my success was the fact that I was competent and caring—possessing the necessary industry knowledge along with a genuine care and concern for my customers.

Meanwhile, as my journey at the publishing company drew to a close, everyone wanted me to ride with them to lunch. These were nice gestures, but I was planning to leave early this day to show property and told them I would have to drive myself. That is when I found out that we were going to a barbeque place by our old office building. I knew then that we were going to the picnic table. They confessed and my heart jumped for joy. I loved this picnic table. It was an amazing day that I will never forget.

The sun was shining when we arrived, and my manager Don was sitting there at the picnic table with all my coworkers. They all were so concerned about it raining, but we sat there rejoicing in the warm sunshine. There was not a raincloud in the sky even though the forecast predicted rain. My manager began to pray, and he too had a word for me—it was almost exactly what my dear friend had told me earlier that morning. Two different people on the same exact day confirming that I was indeed going to reap the rewards of my kindness in helping others.

As Don was closing in prayer, the church bells started to ring at a nearby church. What a wonderful day God had blessed me with, and I would soon be on my way to meet my next adventure as a realtor for God. I will carry with me the memories of this day, and I will keep the verses of Psalm 91 close. These verses have special meaning to me, but I will leave that for another book someday. The verses continue to give me such comfort and peace.

Psalm 91 KJV

1 He that dwelleth in the secret place of the most High shall abide under the shadow of the Almighty.

2 I will say of the LORD, *He is* my refuge and my fortress: my God; in him will I trust.

3 Surely he shall deliver thee from the snare of the fowler, *and* from the noisome pestilence.

4 He shall cover thee with his feathers, and under his wings shalt thou trust: his truth *shall be thy* shield and buckler.

5 Thou shalt not be afraid for the terror by night; *nor* for the arrow *that* flieth by day;

6 *Nor* for the pestilence *that* walketh in darkness; *nor* for the destruction *that* wasteth at noonday.

7 A thousand shall fall at thy side, and ten thousand at thy right hand; *but* it shall not come nigh thee.

8 Only with thine eyes shalt thou behold and see the reward of the wicked.

9 Because thou hast made the LORD, *which is* my refuge, *even* the most High, thy habitation;

10 There shall no evil befall thee, neither shall any plague come nigh thy dwelling.

11 For he shall give his angels charge over thee, to keep thee in all thy ways.

12 They shall bear thee up in *their* hands, lest thou dash thy foot against a stone.

13 Thou shalt tread upon the lion and adder: the young lion and the dragon shalt thou trample under feet.

14 Because he hath set his love upon me, therefore will I deliver him: I will set him on high, because he hath known my name.

15 He shall call upon me, and I will answer him: I *will be* with him in trouble; I will deliver him, and honour him.

16 With long life will I satisfy him, and shew him my salvation.

Photo taken by Don Newman of the original picnic table

Chapter 9

Peace in the Valley

I was soon rushing from my last days on my publishing assignment up I-4 to meet my next assignment as a realtor for God. I would soon learn that I was going to be challenged with this assignment. My challenge consisted of finding one house for two people, but these two people were not in agreement at all.

When the wife, Hannah, and her friend stepped out of the car, it felt as though we had always been friends. We hugged and started talking about her cousin, one of my coworkers, who had referred her to me. They had been looking for a place that was closer to her husband's job. He had been driving from Ocala to Deland for six years, and it was getting harder every day, so I thought for sure they were ready to find a house closer to his job as soon as possible. What I didn't understand was that only he was prepared to make the move.

They had found several homes online that interested them, and they wanted to look at these houses. The very one that Hannah liked already had a contract on it, but I went ahead and showed it to her anyway. I have often wondered since that day if it had not had a contract on it, would it have been the one they chose, but I guess we will never know. As she walked onto the porch she was smitten with the house and its white picket fence. When she saw the kitchen, it was over and she wanted her husband to look at it that very afternoon.

We continued to look at all the other homes, but one in particular really stood out in the group that we had seen. Hannah had to leave and go back to Ocala, so I waited in Deland until her husband, Charles, got off work so he could also view the homes. He was encouraged to think that Hannah was excited about possibly moving, and he rushed over after work to see the home his wife raved about. He instantly knew after walking in the kitchen why she had chosen this home. I assured them that we could try for it, but they both were just not ready to move forward with making an offer.

The following week I received a phone call that Charles wanted to look at the New Smyrna Beach area. I told him it might be a long drive to his work, but he felt it would be an easier drive on a four-lane road instead of the two lanes through the Ocala National

Forest. My husband and I met up with him to view some properties, and he really liked two of them and believed Hannah would like them too. He loved the condo that would allow him to fish right in the backyard. He could not wait for her to see it. The next week we scheduled a time for Hannah to visit; I had several properties for her to view. She did not like the condo at all, but she liked the house in the subdivision better. At the end of the day, she was not feeling well and wanted to head home.

Everything went quiet, and I did not hear from them for a couple of weeks. I was praying for them because I knew Charles was very disappointed that they were not considering the condo. It seemed that they wanted different areas and different houses—there was no common ground where they both agreed. I prayed that God would help me to guide them and asked that He give this husband and wife peace about what to do. Something had to be done because Charles would not and could not continue to drive every day. I was about to find out just how bad the situation was between the two of them when we met at the listing in DeLand by the river.

When we pulled up to the home I was very impressed, but when we walked inside I was even more amazed. The house was so well laid out and so large that it had everything on Hannah's wish list: a garden tub, big closet, and wonderful back patio with pavers. Her friend gushed over how wonderful the house was, but Hannah was finding things that could be changed and pointed these out to her husband. He was still disappointed about not getting the condo, and I could tell he was not in the mood to hear any negativity about this home. Emotions were so taut between the two of them that Hannah's friend felt we should step outside and leave them alone.

I had prayed for peace, and I was having a hard time finding it in this situation, but God is faithful so I continued to try and help them find common ground. Finally, we ended up on the back porch, and that is when God took over. The homeowner returned from her walk with the dog. I asked her how long they had lived at the home; she said they had lived there since they had it built. She loved the home and said she would not be moving except her husband had been commuting to Orlando for a long time, and it was time they made the move to get him closer to his work. The homeowner explained how she felt when the realtor came to put up the sign. Keep in mind the house had only been on the market for about two days. She was still emotionally torn about it, and her son was there with her too. This was the home he had grown up in.

Hannah listened intently as the homeowner poured her heart out. She was in total agreement with how she felt and told her about their dilemma with a decision to move. I stood there thinking *Wow, God has taken care of this, and this will be the home that both the husband and wife agree on!* We left and drove down to look at the river, and still Charles and Hannah were not in agreement. He commented that he would just move to the river and live there, and he might come home and he might not. She said she hoped they would make it to their next anniversary, which was a month away.

I didn't know what to do, but I knew I had to do something. I could plainly see that their marriage was in deep trouble. Taking them both by the hand, I prayed for peace and direction on what they should do about buying and selling. I told them I was writing a book about my adventures as a realtor for God and that they would be featured in a chapter I would call "Peace in the Valley." They both laughed and we waved goodbye, and Hannah called to me from across the parking lot, thanking me for trying to help them. I said, "It's all about the mission, not just the commission!"

In my short time in real estate, I have learned that you decide upon the location first and then you decide on the house. The only thing decided at this point was that Charles wanted to be on the water. We met one more time to view a small condo on the upper portion of the St. Johns River. It needed a lot of work. The next week he called me and wanted to see another condo that was now on the market on the St. John's River. My son and I met him there to view it. My son was familiar with the city and said offhand that no one would want to live there. So we were all pleasantly surprised when I opened the door and it had an amazing view of the river. The price was great too. Charles was ready to move forward but wanted Hannah to view the condo before making an offer. My husband and I returned that same week to show the condo to Hannah. It was finally a peaceful resolution, and with the great price she was able to keep her house that she loved. This condo provided a perfect solution to Charles's long commute.

At first I was concerned that it might place distance between them with him staying there at the river and her at their home in Ocala. This concern faded during the final walk before the closing. I saw how God had restored it all between Charles and Hannah. It was their anniversary, and they were walking from room to room excited about how they would decorate the condo. It was a happy meeting place there by the river. They had told their children about the condo, and now they too were excited about the new home by the river. Hannah also received confirmation from the son that she had made the right decision about not selling the family home. Charles was happy because he got a closer place to his work and now gets to fish instead of making that long drive home.

There was peace in the valley now and happiness on the river! Thank you, Lord!

2 Corinthians 13:11
Finally, brethren, farewell. Be perfect, be of good comfort, be of one mind, live in peace; and the God of love and peace shall be with you.

Matthew 5:9
Blessed are the peacemakers: for they shall be called the children of God.

I made this customized box for them that included a guest book for their guests to write about the special memories made by the river.

Chapter 10

Focused on the Mission

While I was still working in publishing and training to be a realtor, I would receive those emails about the caravans and how the realtors were attending the sales meetings and then visiting the new listings. I longed to attend but knew I had to save every vacation day to show property and attend inspections or closings. There was no time for the fun stuff. That was all about to change.

It was my first week as a full-time realtor for God, and I received an email about a caravan to view a new listing for $2.4 million. In all the previous email notices for caravans, I had never seen one for a home listed at $2.4 million. How sweet it was that God was allowing me to go see this amazing home on my first caravan. It was directly on the ocean and looked like a lighthouse. I thought to myself, *Could it get any better?* We would be viewing the property and then going to lunch with the other realtors in nearby offices. I was so excited about being able to attend this caravan and especially to view this home. It felt good to finally be focused on what God had for my new adventure. I felt like a kid going on a field trip and waited patiently for the day to arrive.

After viewing the house, I wanted to host an open house at this listing and make it very special. This house was huge, with over 7,000 square feet under roof and over 5,000 square feet of heated and air-conditioned space. One of the other realtors had already reserved it for Saturdays, so he agreed that we could share the open house. I baked cookies and bought little fancy crackers. I also spent a lot of time picking out music and making sure that everything was special.

My husband and I woke up early to load the car the following Saturday for the open house. I had packed a lot of stuff, and when we arrived at the house I needed to use the elevator to get up to the main living area. When I stepped inside the elevator and reached for the panel, I saw that someone had labeled the floors creatively. Ground floor was Pearly Gates, the second floor was Heaven, and the third floor was the Promise Land. I could not believe my eyes. I was so excited that when I reached the Heaven floor I asked the other realtor if he too had seen the labels in the elevator. He had not even

Focused On The Mission

noticed them. I told him that it was okay because it was meant for me. I knew it was a confirmation that I was on the path to my calling here on earth. What peace comes from knowing that you're on the right road. You know how you feel when you see the road signs on those long highways that keep confirming you're on the right road. There is peace in knowing that you're not going to have to turn around and repeat your path.

Photo of elevator controls in the house referred to as the Castle!

My job title is realtor, but my primary purpose is sharing the love of God with those He sends my way. I am privileged to be a realtor for God! My job is to show my prospects their earthly homes, but what I feel in my heart is that I am also making sure they have a heavenly home too. In publishing we would call this type of deal a BOGO (Buy One Get One Free). As a realtor for God, I am now helping my clients to purchase a home here on earth while also showing them how to get one in heaven for free. You don't even need a coupon or special code to receive this type of gift. It just doesn't work the same way. All you need is an open heart and acceptance of Jesus Christ as your Lord and Savior. What a wonderful unseen bonus to the house hunters.

John 14:1-4 KJV

1 Let not your heart be troubled: ye believe in God, believe also in me. 2 In my Father's house are many mansions: if *it were* not *so*, I would have told you. I go to prepare a place for you. 3 And if I go and prepare a place for you, I will come again, and receive you unto myself; that where I am, *there* ye may be also. 4 And whither I go ye know, and the way ye know.

This home by the water was what I had envisioned as a heavenly home. I stood amazed each time I got on the elevator and every time I returned to this house. It felt like home. I knew I could not afford to live in this home here on earth, but I will have a more wonderful mansion in heaven. Almost every time I visited I noticed something I had not seen before. It was like a treasure box from God on my new assignment. Two gold-painted gates opened onto the family room, and initially I didn't think about these being the pearly gates in heaven, but over time I came to believe that might be what they represented. When you went through these gates you saw an amazing view of God's beautiful ocean so blue through a whole wall of windows. It took my breath away to watch the sea from an "angel's view" high in the sky from the second- and third-floor levels of this beautiful home. I can only imagine what types of homes I might be showing in heaven if in fact this will be my assignment by God when I get there. All I know for now is that I have a purpose in what I have been assigned to do here on earth, and I love it.

On our last visit to the house it felt different—like it was home. The empty house seemed to be filled. I noticed it when I walked in, and my husband said the same thing. It was a joy to be there with him looking out at the ocean blue. We made plans to return the next day for the open house after church, and I was excited to see who God might send.

Photo taken by Rene Compton –
What a beautiful sandcastle by the sea!

I continue to host other open houses, and my eldest son, Ryan, is kind enough to go with me when my husband is working. What a joy to spend those hours with him. I count this blessing a very special perk. What a fine young man he has become. I am so thankful that he trusts God for wisdom in his life. It brings me joy to introduce him as my son when the visitors arrive. I ask myself again, could this be my new job assignment? It just keeps getting better and better!

3 John 1:4
I have no greater joy than to hear that my children walk in truth.

Daniel 4:3
How great are his signs! and how mighty are his wonders! his kingdom is an everlasting kingdom, and his dominion is from generation to generation.

Chapter 11

Don't Ask Why; Just Go!

As a publishing consultant and writing coach, I spent several years instructing new authors to write the titles of their chapters first. That would allow them to skip around and write what God placed on their heart on any given day, and it also helped them to avoid writer's block. In this manner, they would not be forced to do uninspired writing. I have to laugh at myself because I wrote the title of this chapter and could not for the life of me remember what I intended to write in this chapter. So I deleted it. I went ahead and finished the book, and then it came to me what I had wanted to include. Today it all makes sense, and I can now write this chapter totally inspired and with clarity.

Here goes. A month before I was scheduled to leave the publishing company, one of my coworkers called and said she wanted to go see a house in the Orlando suburbs.

I told her to just let me know when she wanted to go and I would be happy to show it. Later that week one of the Orlando realtors called me up very frustrated because she had to change the showing time on the property for my coworker. She was a bit blunt and asked why I would be showing an Orlando property when I worked out of New Smyrna Beach. I thought it was strange the way she approached me, and I told her that I did show property in this area and currently had one under contract. I explained that I currently worked in Orlando with the client and did not mind setting up the showing with the listing realtor. I apologized to the realtor that my friend had asked her to set up the showing.

I asked the Orlando realtor to give me the street address, but she declined. I was again a bit shocked that she would not at least provide the address, so I called my coworker and she gave me the address. That is when it all made sense. The property was listed at over $1 million, so this realtor was not going to help me to help her. My coworker believed that God wanted her to see this house for some reason and that He wanted me to show it to her. We decided that we would take our lunch hour and go see it. Up to this point, I had never shown a house of this size or price. We were perplexed as to why we might be going to see this house, but my coworker wanted to be obedient to God's prompting.

A portion of the answer was about to be revealed. This showing gave me experience in high-end real estate, and one of the realtors in our office had just signed a contract on an amazing listing—a house referred to as "the castle" that was situated directly on the beach. I was about to host an open house and had invited several of my former coworkers from Orlando to visit, but only one coworker came (the same coworker who believed God wanted her to view the million-dollar home in Orlando with me). I was excited to see what she thought of the castle house.

It was Saturday, and she had attended prayer service earlier that day and then decided to ride over to the beach for a visit. She seemed a bit rushed and was not feeling well. I knew she would be returning to Orlando to go to dinner with another friend, so I dismissed my worry, figuring she was probably just pushed for time. I would find out later what it was.

Lots of unanswered questions surfaced, but soon it would all come together. My husband and I returned to the castle house again for an open house. This was the only time we had been to the home on Sunday after church. Soon we had people coming in, and then my cell phone rang. I picked it up and thought it was my coworker who had visited the previous week, but it was not her. This visitor had come to the door downstairs, but she thought the door was locked and called the number on the side of my car in the driveway. Thankfully, the visitors did not drive away. I met this couple at the door, and it was like I had known them forever. I can't explain it, but I felt as if I were showing the house to a longtime friend. They both loved it and thought it would be a great place for their family. The husband was considering relocating from the mid-south Florida area and wanted to be on the water.

We returned to the entrance area, and I shook the husband's hand. When I reached out my hand to the wife, I found myself hugging her. I am not sure why because this is not something I would typically do at an open house unless someone was my personal friend. It was a bit odd. They left, and I returned to the second level where my husband was sitting. I commented that I needed to keep up with the total number of visitors. As I began counting them, he said I needed to count the people from my previous job too. He thought the couple that called on the phone were the people I knew from work. I then told him about how I felt as though they were friends already.

The next morning, I woke up and envisioned that one of the garage areas would be excellent for their home-based computer business. I could see this house being perfect for them and for their business. As I drove to Orlando for a closing, I decided to reach out to my coworker who had visited the house previously and tell her about these special visitors. That is when she told me she had felt something in the house that was not good the week before when she visited, and that she had prayed and prayed about it when she left. She felt the Lord had cleansed it and prepared it for this couple or its new owners.

I'm not sure what God is going to do with this house or this couple, but I called them to encourage them to look at it one more time. There is something very special about this couple, and I look forward to seeing them again at the castle or at another listing. I look forward to seeing what God has planned.

Chapter 12

Rescue 410

We're all children of God, and we all are different in our own special way. Our all-knowing God provides directions and methods of understanding unique to each individual. Don't feel that your directions from God should be what someone else might experience. All children are not the same, and a good parent or teacher will always adapt their teaching method to that individual child's needs. The most important thing is that they love them just the way they are because God made us all different for a reason and purpose. They look for that child's strengths and then try to keep them interested in pursuing knowledge and understanding to find their path. I believe that God is the perfect parent with the perfect plan for His children. As you read below you will see how God has directed me, His child. His plan is perfect, and I love this Teacher and His divine guidance.

This photograph was taken on April 25, 2017, at 8 p.m. This lifeguard stand is number 410. The numbers 410 came to me at church this past Sunday, July 3, 2017. I began searching my Bible for a verse that could hold some meaning for these numbers, but then I thought about the numbers on the photograph. I couldn't believe it at first, so as soon as church was over I rushed to look at the photo of the lifeguard stand on my phone just to confirm. Even though I had worked long hours trying to reproduce this photo into a painting, I wasn't certain of the numbers on the stand. It might be that when I was painting the numbers, they had just been numbers to me without any significant meaning. Now they meant more. This date, April 10, 2017, was the day God had called me to begin my new journey full-time in real estate! This was the date I was to step out on faith and leave the security of my full-time job and swim out into unknown waters.

This lifeguard stand is just steps away from where I received my instructions from the Lord back in September 2016. I took this picture only because of the beautiful colors reflected in the sunset one afternoon while walking on the beach.

I am now a realtor for God, and He has placed so many confirmations along this journey from the very beginning. This book documents my journey with Him. His encouragement keeps me filled with joy and without fear of the unknown. Nothing is impossible with God. If you open your eyes—and most importantly your heart—to God, He will reveal your path and destiny. He will also be there to encourage you on the path He has chosen for you. Don't let fear hinder what He might be calling you to do. We all have a purpose. Pray and He will show you the way, and He will give you peace on your direction. Don't be afraid to swim into those unknown waters because He will be there to rescue you!

**Photograph taken on 4-25-17 at 8:00 p.m.
by Rene Compton in New Smyrna Beach, FL**

Acrylic Painting - Rescue 410 by Rene Compton

Conclusion

I patiently wait for God to bring every person to me, and then I ask for guidance from the good Lord above. Sometimes the meeting is to teach me new things in life, and other times it is for me to share with others my experiences along my journey. My youngest son said it well this morning. He had called about a concern on his house payment and why it had gone up so much. I spent some time advising him about his escrow and on the plan of action in getting his taxes reviewed by the city, because they had increased so much. I apologized for giving him so much detail, but he patiently replied that he appreciated my guidance and always learns so much from listening to others. Instead of stumbling down the roads of life, he keeps his eyes and ears open. He understands that the Lord provides the wisdom in all things and that God places people in our path to guide us along the way. Being willing to accept this guidance is one of the best keys to success in life!

Proverbs 5:1

My son, attend unto my wisdom, and bow thine ear to my understanding:

Proverbs 2:6

For the LORD giveth wisdom: out of his mouth cometh knowledge and understanding.

Life is an amazing adventure if we only take the time to slow down and enjoy the journey. I feel that I am now on the sightseeing train of life. I revisit those times gone by in my adventurous train ride, and I marvel at what God has done and is doing in my life. And in the lives of my husband and children. How both my sons work right here in New Smyrna Beach. How they trust God in all things. So many miracles in our lives, and so many answered prayers. Every home and every job has a miracle story behind it for each of us. God's hand is on it all, and I pray every day for the safety, wisdom, and favor upon our lives.

I encourage you to take some time today and think back over your life's journey and shine your light on the goodness that God has shown you. Don't travel back down the dark roads that only bring misery and sadness. Believe for the best because that is what God wants for you.

CONCLUSION

It is very important that we stay focused on the mission, which is to guide the lost to their heavenly home. I challenge you today to pray, and if you don't know the Lord that you will ask Him to come into your heart and save you. The Bible teaches us that we all came into this earth as sinners, and we all fall short of God's glory, but God is a merciful God and He will forgive us and save us. Though we all sin at times, God will help us to live a godly lifestyle in a world filled with many temptations. There is no perfect human, and the enemy will try to steal your peace by reminding you of your faults and failures. But you will have the victory when you refuse to listen to the voice of the enemy.

Psalm 72:7
>In his days shall the righteous flourish;
>and abundance of peace so long as the
>moon endureth.

Stay focused and listen to God, and He will show you what He can do through you! You too have a purpose, and it is not just for a beating heart; it is an assignment from God. Ask Him what you might do to make a difference with your life. This is the purpose of life! Just be prepared and go! You can live your life with abundance and peace forever more. He is waiting with your assignment.

Matthew 5:15

    Neither do men light a candle, and put it under a bushel, but on a candlestick; and it giveth light unto all that are in the house.

God loves you so much and He has a plan for your life. Don't miss out on the good life He has waiting for you. The amazing adventures that He has planned. Trust Him the Creator to know the best way to live the life that He has so graciously given you.

"For God so loved the world, that he gave his only begotten Son, that whosoever believeth in him should not perish, but have everlasting life." John 3:16

"For all have sinned, and come short of the glory of God." Romans 3:23

"For the wages of sin is death..." Romans 6:23

"But God commendeth his love toward us, in that, while we were yet sinners, Christ died for us." Romans 5:8

All of our sins were laid on Christ on the cross. He paid our sin debt for us. The Lord Jesus died on the cross, He arose from the dead. He is alive forevermore.

The Bible says, *"For whosoever shall call upon the name of the Lord shall be saved."* Romans 10:13

PRAY AND RECEIVE CHRIST AS YOUR SAVIOR TODAY

Lord, I know I am a sinner. If I died today I would not go to heaven. Forgive my sin, come into my life and be my Savior. Help me live for You from this day forward.

In Jesus' name, Amen

Bible References

https://www.kingjamesbibleonline.org
http://www.bibleinfo.com/en/topics/ten-commandments

Dear Reader,

Thank you for reading Realtor for GOD. I hope that you enjoyed sharing my journey with me. I pray that it will impact not only your life but the lives of others as you share the book with them.

I would love to hear how this book might have touched your heart. How it might have encouraged you in your walk with God. Maybe inspired you to change jobs or look at the opportunity to work for Him in your present job. Most importantly if after reading it that you ask Jesus into your heart. I know this book has purpose but confirmation of it would fill my heart with joy!

If your bookstore, organization or church would like to host a book signing or speaking event please contact me directly either by phone or email. I am planning a book tour and I would like to make your location a part of it. Reserve the date as early as possible!

Your online review on Amazon and Barnes and Nobles is greatly appreciated too!

Phone: (407) 575-2140
Email: renecomptonrealestate@gmail.com

Serving Him by Serving You,

Rene Compton
Realtor for GOD

CPSIA information can be obtained
at www.ICGtesting.com
Printed in the USA
FSOW04n1740051017
39484FS